FAVORITE BRAND NAME™

Publications International, Ltd.

Favorite Brand Name Recipes at www.fbnr.com

Pictured on the front cover: Philadephia® 3-Step® Chocolate Swirl Cheesecake *(page 64)*.

Pictured on the back cover: Cherry Cheesecake Squares *(page 88)*.

Preparation/Cooking Times: Preparation times are based on the approximate amount
of time required to assemble the recipe before cooking, baking, chilling or serving. These
times include preparation steps such as measuring, chopping and mixing. The fact that
some preparations and cooking can be done simultaneously is taken into account.
Preparation of optional ingredients and serving suggestions is not included.

Table of Contents

Irresistible Appetizers

With Philadelphia® Cream Cheese,
creating fabulous appetizers is a snap!
Crowd-pleasing dips, spreads and
other great snacks can be whipped
up in no time.

Baked Cream Cheese Appetizer

1 package (4 ounces) refrigerated crescent dinner rolls
1 package (8 ounces) PHILADELPHIA® Cream Cheese
1/2 teaspoon dill weed
1 egg white, beaten

UNROLL dough on lightly greased cookie sheet; press seams together to form 12×4-inch rectangle.

SPRINKLE top of cream cheese with dill; lightly press dill into cream cheese. Place cream cheese, dill-side up, in center of dough. Bring edges of dough up over cream cheese; press edges of dough together to seal, completely enclosing cream cheese. Brush with egg white.

BAKE at 350°F for 15 to 18 minutes or until lightly browned. Serve with crackers, French bread or cut-up vegetables.   *Makes 8 servings*

Great Substitutes: Try substituting combined 1/2 teaspoon dried rosemary leaves, crushed, and 1/2 teaspoon paprika for the dill weed.

Prep Time: 10 minutes
Bake Time: 18 minutes

Creamy Salsa Dip

1 package (8 ounces) PHILADELPHIA® Cream Cheese, softened
1 cup TACO BELL® HOME ORIGINALS™* Salsa

*TACO BELL and HOME ORIGINALS are registered trademarks owned and licensed by Taco Bell Corp.

MIX cream cheese and salsa until well blended. Refrigerate.

SERVE with tortilla chips or assorted cut-up vegetables.

Makes 2 cups

Prep Time: 10 minutes plus refrigerating

Creamy Salsa Dip

Savory Cheese Ball

1 package (8 ounces) PHILADELPHIA® Cream Cheese, softened

1 package (8 ounces) KRAFT® Shredded Sharp Cheddar Cheese

¾ cup crumbled KRAFT® Natural Blue Cheese

¼ cup chopped green onions

2 tablespoons milk

1 teaspoon Worcestershire sauce

Finely chopped walnuts

MIX cheeses, green onions, milk and Worcestershire sauce until well blended. Refrigerate 1 to 2 hours.

SHAPE into ball; roll in walnuts. Serve with apple and pear slices.

Makes 2⅔ cups

Tip: To make ahead, prepare recipe as directed, but do not roll in nuts. Wrap securely; freeze up to 1 month. Roll in nuts just before serving. (Note: A slight texture change may be noticed.)

Great Substitutes: Substitute finely chopped pecans or almonds for walnuts.

Prep Time: 5 minutes plus refrigerating

Pesto Christmas Tree

1 package (8 ounces) PHILADELPHIA® Cream Cheese
$^1/_3$ cup DI GIORNO® Pesto
Cinnamon stick

CUT cream cheese in half diagonally. Place triangles together to form Christmas tree shape on serving plate.

TOP with pesto. Insert cinnamon stick at base of triangle for "tree trunk." Serve with crackers.   *Makes 12 servings*

Tip: Use chopped red pepper as "ornaments" to decorate tree.

Prep Time: 5 minutes

Philadelphia® Onion Dip

1 package (8 ounces) PHILADELPHIA® Cream Cheese, softened
3 tablespoons milk
2 tablespoons onion soup mix

MIX cream cheese and milk with electric mixer on medium speed until smooth.

BLEND in soup mix. Refrigerate. Serve with assorted cut-up vegetables or chips.   *Makes 1 cup*

Prep Time: 5 minutes plus refrigerating

Pesto Christmas Tree

Chili Cheese Dip

1 package (8 ounces) PHILADELPHIA® Cream Cheese, softened
1 can (15 ounces) chili with *or* without beans
1 cup KRAFT® Shredded Cheddar Cheese

SPREAD cream cheese onto bottom and up sides of 9-inch microwavable pie plate or quiche dish. Spread chili over cream cheese. Sprinkle with cheddar cheese.

MICROWAVE on HIGH 3 minutes or until thoroughly heated.

SERVE hot with tortilla chips.   *Makes 3 cups*

Prep Time: 5 minutes
Microwave Time: 3 minutes

Chili Cheese Dip

Zesty Shrimp Spread

1 package (8 ounces) PHILADELPHIA® Cream Cheese, softened

$^{1}/_{2}$ cup KRAFT® Mayo Real Mayonnaise

1 cup chopped, cooked, cleaned shrimp

$^{1}/_{4}$ cup KRAFT® 100% Grated Parmesan Cheese

2 tablespoons chopped fresh parsley *or* cilantro

2 cloves garlic, minced

BEAT cream cheese and mayo with electric mixer on medium speed until well blended.

ADD remaining ingredients; mix well. Refrigerate.

SERVE with crackers or toasted bread rounds.   *Makes 2$^{1}/_{4}$ cups*

Prep Time: 5 minutes plus refrigerating

Party Cheese Wreath

2 packages (8 ounces each) PHILADELPHIA® Cream Cheese, softened
1 package (8 ounces) KRAFT® Shredded Sharp Cheddar Cheese
1 tablespoon chopped red pepper
1 tablespoon finely chopped onion
2 teaspoons Worcestershire sauce
1 teaspoon lemon juice
  Dash ground red pepper

MIX cream cheese and cheddar cheese with electric mixer on medium speed until well blended.

BLEND in remaining ingredients. Refrigerate several hours or overnight.

PLACE drinking glass in center of serving platter. Drop round tablespoonfuls of cheese mixture around glass, just touching outer edge of glass to form ring; smooth with spatula. Remove glass. Garnish with chopped fresh parsley and additional chopped red pepper. Serve with crackers.   *Makes 12 servings*

Mini Cheese Balls: Shape cream cheese mixture into 1-inch balls. Roll in light rye bread crumbs or dark pumpernickel bread crumbs.

Prep Time: 15 minutes plus refrigerating

Party Cheese Wreath

Spinach Cheese Triangles

1 package (8 ounces) PHILADELPHIA® Cream Cheese, softened

1 package (10 ounces) frozen chopped spinach, thawed, well drained

$^1/_3$ cup chopped drained roasted red peppers

$^1/_4$ teaspoon garlic salt

6 sheets frozen phyllo, thawed

$^1/_2$ cup (1 stick) butter or margarine, melted

MIX cream cheese, spinach, red peppers and garlic salt with electric mixer on medium speed until well blended.

LAY 1 phyllo sheet on flat surface. Brush with some of the melted butter. Cut lengthwise into 4 ($18 \times 3^1/_2$-inch) strips.

SPOON about 1 tablespoon filling about 1 inch from one end of each strip. Fold the end over the filling at a 45-degree angle. Continue folding as you would fold a flag to form a triangle that encloses filling. Repeat procedure with remaining phyllo sheets. Place triangles on cookie sheet. Brush with melted butter.

BAKE at 375°F for 12 to 15 minutes or until golden brown.

Makes 3 dozen appetizers

Tip: Unfold phyllo sheets; cover with wax paper and damp towel to prevent drying until ready to use.

Prep Time: 30 minutes
Bake Time: 15 minutes

Creamy Feta & Sun-Dried Tomato Spread

1 package (8 ounces) PHILADELPHIA® Cream Cheese, softened

1 package (4 ounces) ATHENOS® Crumbled Feta Cheese

2 tablespoons chopped fresh basil

2 tablespoons finely chopped sun-dried tomatoes

MIX all ingredients. Refrigerate.

SERVE as a spread on crackers or fresh vegetables.   *Makes 1½ cups*

Prep Time: 10 minutes plus refrigerating

Creamy Feta & Sun-Dried Tomato Spread

Three Pepper Quesadillas

1 cup *each* thin green, red and yellow pepper strips

$1/2$ cup thin onion slices

$1/2$ teaspoon ground cumin

$1/3$ cup butter *or* margarine

1 package (8 ounces) PHILADELPHIA® Cream Cheese, softened

1 package (8 ounces) KRAFT® Shredded Sharp Cheddar Cheese

10 flour tortillas (6 inch)

TACO BELL® HOME ORIGINALS™* Salsa

TACO BELL and HOME ORIGINALS are registered trademarks owned and licensed by Taco Bell Corp.

COOK and stir peppers, onion and cumin in butter in large skillet until tender-crisp, about 4 minutes. Drain, reserving butter.

MIX cream cheese and cheddar cheese until well blended. Spoon 2 tablespoons cheese mixture onto each tortilla; top with scant $1/3$ cup pepper mixture. Fold tortillas in half; place on cookie sheet. Brush with reserved butter.

BAKE at 425°F for 10 minutes. Cut each tortilla into thirds. Serve warm with salsa. *Makes 30 appetizers*

To Make Ahead: Prepare as directed except for baking; cover. Refrigerate. When ready to serve, bake, uncovered, at 425°F, 15 to 20 minutes.

Prep Time: 20 minutes
Bake Time: 10 minutes

Three Pepper Quesadillas

Bacon Appetizer Crescents

1 package (8 ounces) PHILADELPHIA® Cream Cheese, softened

½ cup OSCAR MAYER® Bacon Bits *or* 8 slices OSCAR MAYER®
        Bacon, crisply cooked, crumbled

⅓ cup KRAFT® 100% Grated Parmesan Cheese

¼ cup thinly sliced green onions

1 tablespoon milk

2 cans (8 ounces each) refrigerated crescent dinner rolls
    Poppy seed (optional)

MIX cream cheese, bacon bits, Parmesan cheese, onions and milk until well blended.

SEPARATE dough into 8 rectangles; firmly press perforations together to seal. Spread each rectangle with 2 rounded tablespoonfuls cream cheese mixture.

CUT each rectangle in half diagonally; repeat with opposite corners. Cut in half crosswise to form 6 triangles. Roll up triangles, starting at short ends. Place on ungreased cookie sheets. Sprinkle with poppy seed.

BAKE at 375°F for 12 to 15 minutes or until golden brown. Serve immediately. *Makes 4 dozen*

Prep Time: 30 minutes
Bake Time: 15 minutes

Roasted Red Pepper Pesto Cheesecake

1 cup butter-flavored cracker crumbs (about 40 crackers)

$^1\!/_4$ cup ($^1\!/_2$ stick) butter *or* margarine, melted

2 packages (8 ounces each) PHILADELPHIA® Cream Cheese, softened

1 cup ricotta cheese

3 eggs

$^1\!/_2$ cup KRAFT® 100% Grated Parmesan Cheese

$^1\!/_2$ cup DI GIORNO® Pesto

$^1\!/_2$ cup drained roasted red peppers, puréed

MIX crumbs and butter. Press onto bottom of 9-inch springform pan. Bake at 325°F for 10 minutes.

MIX cream cheese and ricotta cheese with electric mixer on medium speed until well blended. Add eggs, 1 at a time, mixing well after each addition. Blend in remaining ingredients. Pour over crust.

BAKE at 325°F for 55 minutes to 1 hour or until center is almost set. Run knife or metal spatula around rim of pan to loosen cake; cool before removing rim of pan. Refrigerate 4 hours or overnight. Let stand at room temperature 15 minutes before serving. Store leftover cheesecake in refrigerator.   *Makes 12 to 14 servings*

Prep Time: 15 minutes plus refrigerating
Bake Time: 1 hour plus standing

Black Bean Spirals

4 ounces PHILADELPHIA® Cream Cheese, softened

1/2 cup (2 ounces) KRAFT® Mexican Style Finely Shredded
Cheddar and Monterey Jack Cheese with Jalapeño Peppers*

1/4 cup BREAKSTONE'S® or KNUDSEN® Sour Cream

1/4 teaspoon onion salt

1 cup canned black beans, rinsed, drained

3 (10-inch) flour tortillas

Salsa

*May also use KRAFT Shredded Monterey Jack Cheese.

MIX cheeses, sour cream and onion salt with electric mixer on medium
speed until well blended.

PLACE beans in food processor container fitted with steel blade or
blender container; cover. Process until smooth. Spread thin layer of
beans on each tortilla; spread cheese mixture over beans.

ROLL tortillas up tightly. Refrigerate 30 minutes. Cut into 1/2-inch
slices. Serve with salsa.   *Makes 10 servings*

Prep Time: 15 minutes plus refrigerating

*For a change of pace and an
extra burst of color, try using
flavored flour tortillas, such as
spinach or tomato, in addition
to plain ones when you prepare
these spirals.*

Black Bean Spirals

Creamy Pesto Dip

1 package (8 ounces) PHILADELPHIA® Cream Cheese, softened
3 tablespoons milk
1/3 cup DI GIORNO® Basil Pesto Sauce
1 red pepper, finely chopped (about 1 cup)

MIX cream cheese and milk with electric mixer on medium speed until smooth. Blend in pesto and red pepper. Refrigerate.

SERVE with assorted cut-up vegetables, breadsticks or chips.

Makes about 2 1/3 cups

Prep Time: 5 minutes plus refrigerating

Creamy Pesto Dip

Southwestern Cheesecake

1 cup finely crushed tortilla chips

3 tablespoons butter *or* margarine, melted

2 packages (8 ounces) PHILADELPHIA® Cream Cheese,
    softened

2 eggs

1 package (8 ounces) KRAFT® Shredded Colby/Monterey Jack
    Cheese

1 (4-ounce) can chopped green chilies, drained

1 cup BREAKSTONE'S® *or* KNUDSEN® Sour Cream

1 cup chopped yellow *or* orange pepper

1/2 cup green onion slices

1/3 cup chopped tomatoes

1/4 cup sliced pitted ripe olives

MIX chips and butter in small bowl; press onto bottom of 9-inch springform pan. Bake at 325°F for 15 minutes.

BEAT cream cheese and eggs at medium speed with electric mixer until well blended. Mix in shredded cheese and chilies; pour over crust. Bake for 30 minutes.

SPREAD sour cream over cheesecake. Loosen cake from rim of pan; cool before removing rim of pan. Chill.

TOP with remaining ingredients just before serving.

Makes 16 to 20 appetizer servings

Prep Time: 20 minutes plus refrigerating
Bake Time: 30 minutes

7-Layer Mexican Dip

1 package (8 ounces) PHILADELPHIA® Cream Cheese, softened

1 tablespoon TACO BELL® HOME ORIGINALS™* Taco
  Seasoning Mix

1 cup *each* guacamole, TACO BELL® HOME ORIGINALS™
  Salsa and shredded lettuce

1 cup KRAFT® Shredded Mild Cheddar Cheese

1/2 cup chopped green onions

2 tablespoons sliced pitted ripe olives

TACO BELL and HOME ORIGINALS are registered trademarks owned and licensed by Taco Bell Corp.

MIX cream cheese and seasoning mix. Spread onto bottom of 9-inch pie plate or quiche dish.

LAYER guacamole, salsa, lettuce, cheddar cheese, onions and olives over cream cheese mixture. Refrigerate.

SERVE with tortilla chips.   *Makes 6 to 8 servings*

Great Substitutes: If your family doesn't like guacamole, try substituting 1 cup TACO BELL® HOME ORIGINALS™ Refried Beans.

Prep Time: 10 minutes plus refrigerating

7-Layer Mexican Dip

Savory Bruschetta

 ¹/₄ cup olive oil
 1 clove garlic, minced
 1 loaf (1 pound) French bread, cut in half lengthwise
 1 package (8 ounces) PHILADELPHIA® Cream Cheese, softened
 3 tablespoons KRAFT® 100% Grated Parmesan Cheese
 2 tablespoons chopped pitted Niçoise olives
 1 cup chopped plum tomatoes
 Fresh basil leaves

MIX oil and garlic; spread on cut surfaces of bread. Bake at 400°F for 8 to 10 minutes or until toasted. Cool.

MIX cream cheese and Parmesan cheese with electric mixer on medium speed until blended. Stir in olives. Spread on cooled bread halves.

TOP with tomatoes and basil leaves. Cut into slices.   *Makes 2 dozen*

Prep Time: 15 minutes
Bake Time: 10 minutes

*Niçoise olives are small, oval-shaped olives that come
from France's Provence region. They are cured in
brine and packed in olive oil, and they are available at
many supermarkets and specialty stores.*

Savory Bruschetta

Hot Artichoke Dip

1 package (8 ounces) PHILADELPHIA® Cream Cheese, softened
1 can (14 ounces) artichoke hearts, drained, chopped
$^1/_2$ cup KRAFT® Mayo Real Mayonnaise
$^1/_2$ cup KRAFT® 100% Grated Parmesan Cheese
1 clove garlic, minced

MIX all ingredients with electric mixer on medium speed until well blended. Spoon into 9-inch pie plate or quiche dish.

BAKE at 350°F for 20 to 25 minutes or until very lightly browned.

SERVE with vegetable dippers or baked pita bread wedges.

Makes 2$^1/_2$ cups

Special Extras: To make baked pita bread wedges, cut each of 3 split pita breads into 8 triangles. Place on cookie sheet. Bake at 350°F for 10 to 12 minutes or until crisp.

Prep Time: 15 minutes
Bake Time: 25 minutes

To soften cream cheese quickly, place an unwrapped
package of cream cheese on a microwavable plate.
Microwave on HIGH (100% power) for 15 seconds.

Hot Artichoke Dip

Easy Entrées & Sides

Great meals don't have to be time-consuming to prepare. Family favorites like Chicken Enchiladas and Easy Fettuccine Alfredo are surprisingly—and deliciously—simple.

Chicken Enchiladas

2 cups chopped cooked chicken *or* turkey

1 cup chopped green pepper

1 package (8 ounces) PHILADELPHIA® Cream Cheese, cubed

1 jar (8 ounces) salsa, divided

8 (6-inch) flour tortillas

¾ pound (12 ounces) VELVEETA® Pasteurized Process Cheese
   Spread, cut up

¼ cup milk

STIR chicken, pepper, cream cheese and ½ cup salsa in saucepan on low heat until cream cheese is melted.

SPOON ⅓ cup chicken mixture down center of each tortilla; roll up. Place, seam-side down, in lightly greased 12×8-inch baking dish.

STIR process cheese spread and milk in saucepan on low heat until smooth. Pour sauce over tortillas; cover with foil.

BAKE at 350°F for 20 minutes or until thoroughly heated. Pour remaining salsa over tortillas.   *Makes 4 to 6 servings*

Prep Time: 20 minutes
Bake Time: 20 minutes

Layered Orange Pineapple Mold

1 can (20 ounces) crushed pineapple in juice, undrained
  Cold water
1 ½ cups boiling water
1 package (8-serving size) *or* 2 packages (4-serving size) JELL-O®
  Brand Orange Flavor Gelatin Dessert
1 package (8 ounces) PHILADELPHIA® Cream Cheese, softened

DRAIN pineapple, reserving juice. Add cold water to juice to make 1 ½ cups.

STIR boiling water into gelatin in large bowl at least 2 minutes until completely dissolved. Stir in measured pineapple juice and water. Reserve 1 cup gelatin at room temperature.

STIR ½ of the crushed pineapple into remaining gelatin. Pour into 6-cup mold. Refrigerate about 2 hours or until set but not firm (gelatin should stick to finger when touched and should mound).

STIR reserved 1 cup gelatin gradually into cream cheese in medium bowl with wire whisk until smooth. Stir in remaining crushed pineapple. Pour over gelatin layer in mold.

REFRIGERATE 4 hours or until firm. Unmold. Garnish as desired.

Makes 10 servings

Prep Time: 20 minutes
Refrigerating Time: 6 hours

Layered Orange Pineapple Mold

Seafood Quiche

1 package (8 ounces) PHILADELPHIA® Cream Cheese, softened
1 can (6 ounces) crabmeat, drained, flaked
4 eggs
1/2 cup sliced green onions
1/2 cup milk
1/2 teaspoon dill weed
1/2 teaspoon lemon and pepper seasoning salt
1 (9-inch) baked pastry shell

MIX all ingredients except pastry shell with electric mixer on medium speed until well blended.

POUR into pastry shell.

BAKE at 350°F for 40 minutes or until knife inserted in center comes out clean. Let stand 10 minutes before serving.   *Makes 6 to 8 servings*

Serving Suggestion: For a luncheon or light dinner, serve with fresh-cut melon slices.

Prep Time: 15 minutes
Bake Time: 40 minutes plus standing

Seafood Quiche

Philadelphia® Mashed Potatoes

6 cups (2 pounds) peeled quartered potatoes

$^{1}/_{2}$ cup milk

1 package (8 ounces) PHILADELPHIA® Cream Cheese, softened

$^{1}/_{2}$ teaspoon onion powder

$^{1}/_{2}$ to $^{3}/_{4}$ teaspoon salt

$^{1}/_{4}$ teaspoon pepper

Paprika

PLACE potatoes and enough water to cover in 3-quart saucepan. Bring to boil. Reduce heat to medium; cook 20 to 25 minutes or until tender. Drain.

MASH potatoes, gradually stirring in milk, cream cheese, onion powder, salt and pepper until light and fluffy. Sprinkle with paprika. Serve immediately.   *Makes 8 servings*

To Make Ahead: Prepare as directed. Spoon into $1^{1}/_{2}$-quart casserole; cover. Refrigerate overnight. When ready to serve, bake, uncovered, at 350°F for 1 hour or until thoroughly heated.

Prep Time: 10 minutes
Cook Time: 30 minutes

Easy Fettuccine Alfredo

1 package (8 ounces) PHILADELPHIA® Cream Cheese, cubed
1 cup (4 ounces) KRAFT® Shredded Parmesan Cheese
½ cup (1 stick) butter *or* margarine
½ cup milk
8 ounces fettuccine, cooked, drained

STIR cream cheese, Parmesan cheese, butter and milk in large saucepan on low heat until smooth.

ADD fettuccine; toss lightly. Serve with additional Parmesan cheese, if desired.   *Makes 4 servings*

Creamed Spinach Casserole

2 packages (10 ounces each) frozen chopped spinach, thawed, well drained
2 packages (8 ounces each) PHILADELPHIA® Cream Cheese, softened
1 teaspoon lemon and pepper seasoning salt
⅓ cup crushed seasoned croutons

MIX spinach, cream cheese and seasoning salt until well blended.

SPOON mixture into 1-quart casserole. Sprinkle with crushed croutons.

BAKE at 350°F for 25 to 30 minutes or until thoroughly heated.
                                    Makes 6 to 8 servings

Prep Time: 10 minutes
Bake Time: 30 minutes

Chicken in Cream Sauce

4 boneless skinless chicken breast halves (about 1¼ pounds),
    cut into strips
1 medium red pepper, cut into strips
¼ cup sliced green onions
1 teaspoon Italian seasoning
½ teaspoon salt
2 tablespoons butter *or* margarine
¼ cup dry white wine, divided
1 package (8 ounces) PHILADELPHIA® Cream Cheese, cubed
½ cup milk
8 ounces linguine, cooked, drained

COOK chicken, vegetables and seasonings in butter in medium skillet on medium heat 10 minutes or until chicken is cooked through, stirring occasionally. Add 2 tablespoons wine; simmer 5 minutes.

STIR cream cheese, milk and remaining 2 tablespoons wine in small saucepan on low heat until smooth.

PLACE hot linguine on serving platter; top with chicken mixture and cream cheese mixture. Garnish, if desired.   *Makes 4 to 6 servings*

Prep Time: 20 minutes
Cook Time: 20 minutes

Chicken in Cream Sauce

Layered Pear Cream Cheese Mold

1 can (16 ounces) pear halves, undrained
1 package (8-serving size) *or* 2 packages (4-serving size) JELL-O®
    Brand Lime Flavor Gelatin Dessert
1¹/₂ cups cold ginger ale *or* water
2 tablespoons lemon juice
1 package (8 ounces) PHILADELPHIA® Cream Cheese, softened
¹/₄ cup chopped pecans

DRAIN pears, reserving liquid. Dice pears; set aside. Add water to liquid to make 1¹/₂ cups; bring to boil in small saucepan.

STIR boiling liquid into gelatin in large bowl at least 2 minutes until completely dissolved. Stir in cold ginger ale and lemon juice. Reserve 2¹/₂ cups gelatin at room temperature. Pour remaining gelatin into 5-cup mold. Refrigerate about 30 minutes or until thickened (spoon drawn through leaves definite impression). Arrange about ¹/₂ cup of the diced pears in thickened gelatin in mold.

STIR reserved 2¹/₂ cups gelatin gradually into cream cheese in large bowl with wire whisk until smooth. Refrigerate about 30 minutes or until slightly thickened (consistency of unbeaten egg whites). Stir in remaining diced pears and pecans. Spoon over gelatin layer in mold.

REFRIGERATE 4 hours or until firm. Unmold. Garnish as desired.

Makes 10 servings

Prep Time: 30 minutes
Refrigerating Time: 5 hours

Layered Pear Cream Cheese Mold

Under-the-Sea Salad

1 can (16 ounces) pear halves in syrup, undrained

1 cup boiling water

1 package (4-serving size) JELL-O® Brand Lime Flavor Gelatin
   Dessert

1/4 teaspoon salt (optional)

1 tablespoon lemon juice

3 packages (3 ounces each) PHILADELPHIA® Cream Cheese,
   softened

1/8 teaspoon ground cinnamon (optional)

DRAIN pears, reserving 3/4 cup of the syrup. Dice pears; set aside.

STIR boiling water into gelatin and salt in medium bowl at least
2 minutes until completely dissolved. Stir in reserved syrup and lemon
juice. Pour 1 1/4 cups gelatin into 4-cup mold or 8×4-inch loaf pan.
Refrigerate about 1 hour or until set but not firm (gelatin should stick to
finger when touched and should mound).

MEANWHILE, stir remaining gelatin gradually into cream cheese in
large bowl with wire whisk until smooth. Stir in pears and cinnamon.
Spoon over gelatin layer in mold.

REFRIGERATE 4 hours or until firm. Unmold. Garnish as desired.

Makes 6 servings

Prep Time: 20 minutes
Refrigerating Time: 5 hours

Sweet Potato Crisp

1 can (40 ounces) cut sweet potatoes, drained

1 package (8 ounces) PHILADELPHIA® Cream Cheese, softened

³/₄ cup firmly packed brown sugar, divided

¹/₄ teaspoon ground cinnamon

1 cup chopped apples

²/₃ cup chopped cranberries

¹/₂ cup flour

¹/₂ cup old-fashioned *or* quick-cooking oats, uncooked

¹/₃ cup butter *or* margarine

¹/₄ cup chopped pecans

MIX sweet potatoes, cream cheese, ¹/₄ cup of the sugar and cinnamon with electric mixer on medium speed until well blended. Spoon into 1¹/₂-quart casserole or 10×6-inch baking dish. Top with apples and cranberries.

MIX flour, oats and remaining ¹/₂ cup sugar in medium bowl; cut in butter until mixture resembles coarse crumbs. Stir in pecans. Sprinkle over fruit.

BAKE at 350°F for 35 to 40 minutes or until thoroughly heated.

Makes 8 servings

Prep Time: 20 minutes
Bake Time: 40 minutes

Twice-Baked Potatoes

   4 large baking potatoes, baked
   1 package (8 ounces) PHILADELPHIA® Cream Cheese, softened
$^1/_3$ cup milk
$^1/_2$ teaspoon salt
   Dash pepper
$^1/_4$ cup chopped green onions
   Paprika

CUT potatoes in half lengthwise; scoop out centers, leaving $^1/_8$-inch shell.

MASH potatoes and cream cheese. Add milk and seasonings; beat until fluffy. Stir in onions; spoon into shells. Place on cookie sheet. Sprinkle with paprika.

BAKE at 350°F for 20 to 25 minutes or until thoroughly heated.

Makes 8 servings

Twice-Baked Potato

Chicken Tetrazzini

$^1/_2$ cup chopped onion

$^1/_2$ cup chopped celery

$^1/_4$ cup ($^1/_2$ stick) butter *or* margarine

1 can (13$^3/_4$ ounces) chicken broth

1 package (8 ounces) PHILADELPHIA® Cream Cheese, cubed

$^3/_4$ cup (3 ounces) KRAFT® 100% Grated Parmesan Cheese,
     divided

1 package (7 ounces) spaghetti, cooked, drained

1 jar (6 ounces) whole mushrooms, drained

1 cup chopped cooked chicken *or* turkey

COOK and stir onion and celery in butter in large skillet on medium heat until tender. Add broth, cream cheese and $^1/_2$ cup Parmesan cheese; stir on low heat until cream cheese is melted.

ADD remaining ingredients except remaining Parmesan cheese; toss lightly. Spoon into 12×8-inch baking dish; sprinkle with remaining $^1/_4$ cup Parmesan cheese.

BAKE at 350°F for 30 minutes.   *Makes 6 servings*

Prep Time: 20 minutes

Bake Time: 30 minutes

Cheesecake Heaven

Caramel Pecan, Cookies and Cream, Luscious Lemon.... it can be so difficult to choose a cheesecake! But whatever your choice, you'll find they're all easy to make—and impossible to resist.

Classic New York Cheesecake

CRUST
    1 cup graham cracker crumbs
    3 tablespoons sugar
    3 tablespoons butter *or* margarine, melted

FILLING
    4 packages (8 ounces each) PHILADELPHIA® Cream Cheese,
        softened
    1 cup sugar
    3 tablespoons flour
    1 tablespoon vanilla
    1 cup BREAKSTONE'S® *or* KNUDSEN® Sour Cream
    4 eggs

CRUST
MIX crumbs, sugar and butter; press onto bottom of 9-inch springform
pan. Bake at 325°F for 10 minutes if using a silver springform pan.
(Bake at 300°F for 10 minutes if using a dark nonstick springform pan.)

FILLING
MIX cream cheese, sugar, flour and vanilla with electric mixer on medium
speed until well blended. Blend in sour cream. Add eggs, mixing on low
speed just until blended. Pour over crust.

BAKE at 325°F for 65 to 70 minutes or until center is almost set
if using a silver springform pan. (Bake at 300°F for 65 to 70 minutes if
using a dark nonstick springform pan.) Run knife or metal spatula around
rim of pan to loosen cake; cool before removing rim of pan. Refrigerate
4 hours or overnight.   *Makes 12 servings*

Philadelphia® 3-Step® Fruit Topped Cheesecake

2 packages (8 ounces each) PHILADELPHIA® Cream Cheese, softened

$^{1}/_{2}$ cup sugar

$^{1}/_{2}$ teaspoon vanilla

2 eggs

1 ready-to-use graham cracker pie crust (6 ounces or 9 inch)

2 cups sliced fresh fruit slices

2 tablespoons strawberry *or* apple jelly, heated (optional)

MIX cream cheese, sugar and vanilla with electric mixer on medium speed until well blended. Add eggs; mix until blended.

POUR into crust.

BAKE at 350°F for 40 minutes or until center is almost set. Cool. Refrigerate 3 hours or overnight. Top with fruit; drizzle with jelly, if desired.   *Makes 8 servings*

Prep Time: 10 minutes
Bake Time: 40 minutes

To prevent cheesecakes from cracking, be careful not to overbeat the batter. Beat at low speed after adding the eggs, just until blended. Fold in any additional ingredients gently.

Philadelphia® 3-Step® Fruit Topped Cheesecake

Autumn Cheesecake

CRUST

1 cup graham cracker crumbs

$^1/_2$ cup finely chopped pecans

3 tablespoons sugar

$^1/_2$ teaspoon ground cinnamon

$^1/_4$ cup ($^1/_2$ stick) butter *or* margarine, melted

FILLING

2 packages (8 ounces each) PHILADELPHIA® Cream Cheese,
    softened

$^1/_2$ cup sugar

$^1/_2$ teaspoon vanilla

2 eggs

TOPPING

$^1/_3$ cup sugar

$^1/_2$ teaspoon ground cinnamon

4 cups thinly sliced peeled apples

$^1/_4$ cup finely chopped pecans

CRUST

MIX crumbs, pecans, sugar, cinnamon and butter; press onto bottom of 9-inch springform pan. Bake at 325°F for 10 minutes if using a silver springform pan. (Bake at 300°F for 10 minutes if using a dark nonstick springform pan.)

FILLING

MIX cream cheese, sugar and vanilla with mixer on medium speed until blended. Add eggs; mix on low speed just until blended. Pour over crust.

TOPPING

MIX sugar and cinnamon; toss with apples. Spoon apple mixture over cream cheese layer; sprinkle with pecans.

BAKE at 325°F for 1 hour and 10 minutes to 1 hour and 15 minutes or until center is almost set if using a silver springform pan. (Bake at 300°F for 1 hour and 10 minutes to 1 hour and 15 minutes or until center is almost set if using a dark nonstick springform pan.) Run knife or metal spatula around rim of pan to loosen cake; cool before removing rim of pan. Refrigerate 4 hours or overnight. *Makes 12 servings*

Prep Time: 25 minutes plus refrigerating
Bake Time: 1 hour 15 minutes

Autumn Cheesecake

Philadelphia® 3-Step® Luscious Lemon Cheesecake

2 packages (8 ounces each) PHILADELPHIA® Cream Cheese, softened

$^{1}/_{2}$ cup sugar

1 tablespoon fresh lemon juice

$^{1}/_{2}$ teaspoon grated lemon peel

$^{1}/_{2}$ teaspoon vanilla

2 eggs

1 ready-to-use graham cracker crumb crust (6 ounces or 9 inch)

MIX cream cheese, sugar, juice, peel and vanilla with electric mixer on medium speed until well blended. Add eggs; mix until blended.

POUR into crust.

BAKE at 350°F for 40 minutes or until center is almost set. Cool. Refrigerate 3 hours or overnight. Garnish with COOL WHIP® Whipped Topping and lemon slices.   *Makes 8 servings*

Prep Time: 10 minutes
Bake Time: 40 minutes

One medium-size lemon will yield about 3 to 4 tablespoons of juice and 1 to 2 teaspoons of grated peel.

Philadelphia® 3-Step® Luscious Lemon Cheesecake

Caramel Brownie Cheesecake

1 (8-ounce) package brownie mix

1 egg

1 tablespoon cold water

1 (14-ounce) bag caramels

1 (5-ounce) can evaporated milk

2 packages (8 ounces each) PHILADELPHIA® Cream Cheese, softened

$^1/_2$ cup sugar

1 teaspoon vanilla

2 eggs

KRAFT® Chocolate Topping

MIX together brownie mix, 1 egg and water in medium bowl until well blended. Spread into greased 9-inch square baking pan. Bake at 350°F for 25 minutes.

MELT caramels with milk in heavy $1^1/_2$-quart saucepan over low heat, stirring frequently until smooth. Reserve $^1/_3$ cup caramel mixture for topping. Pour remaining caramel mixture over crust.

BEAT cream cheese, sugar and vanilla in large mixing bowl at medium speed with electric mixer until well blended.

ADD 2 eggs, one at a time, mixing well after each addition. Pour over caramel mixture in pan.

BAKE for 40 minutes; cool. Chill.

HEAT reserved caramel mixture in small saucepan until warm. Spoon over cheesecake. Drizzle with chocolate topping.

Makes 12 to 16 servings

Variations: Substitute 9-inch springform pan for square baking pan. Loosen cake from rim of pan before cooling.

Microwave Directions: To melt caramels, microwave caramels with milk in small deep glass bowl on HIGH $2\frac{1}{2}$ to $3\frac{1}{2}$ minutes or until sauce is smooth when stirred, stirring after each minute.

Fluffy 2-Step Cheesecake

> 2 packages (8 ounces each) PHILADELPHIA® Cream Cheese, softened
> $\frac{1}{3}$ cup sugar
> 1 tub (8 ounces) COOL WHIP® Whipped Topping, thawed
> 1 ready-to-use graham cracker crumb crust (6 ounces or 9 inch)

MIX cream cheese and sugar in large bowl with electric mixer on medium speed until smooth. Gently stir in whipped topping.

SPOON into crust. Refrigerate 3 hours or until set. Top with fresh fruit or cherry pie filling, if desired. Store leftover cheesecake in refrigerator.

Makes 8 servings

Prep Time: 15 minutes plus refrigerating

Philadelphia® 3-Step® Mini Cheesecakes

2 packages (8 ounces each) PHILADELPHIA® Cream Cheese, softened

$^1/_2$ cup sugar

$^1/_2$ teaspoon vanilla

2 eggs

2 packages (4 ounces each) KEEBLER® READY CRUST Single Serve Graham Cracker Pie Crusts

MIX cream cheese, sugar and vanilla with electric mixer on medium speed until well blended. Add eggs; mix until blended.

POUR into crusts placed on cookie sheets.

BAKE at 350°F for 20 minutes or until centers are almost set. Cool. Refrigerate 3 hours or overnight. Garnish with fresh fruit.

Makes 12 servings

Prep Time: 10 minutes
Bake Time: 20 minutes

Philadelphia® 3-Step® Mini Cheesecakes

Philadelphia® 3-Step® Caramel Apple Cheesecake

2 packages (8 ounces each) PHILADELPHIA® Cream Cheese, softened

$^1/_2$ cup sugar

$^1/_2$ teaspoon vanilla

2 eggs

$^1/_3$ cup frozen apple juice concentrate, thawed

1 ready-to-use graham cracker crust (6 ounces or 9 inch)

$^1/_4$ cup caramel ice cream topping

$^1/_4$ cup chopped peanuts

MIX cream cheese, sugar and vanilla at medium speed with electric mixer until well blended. Add eggs; mix until blended. Blend in juice concentrate.

POUR into crust.

BAKE at 350°F for 40 minutes or until center is almost set. Cool. Refrigerate 3 hours or overnight. Drizzle with topping and sprinkle with peanuts before serving. Garnish with apple slices.   *Makes 8 servings*

Prep Time: 10 minutes
Bake Time: 40 minutes

Philadelphia® 3-Step® Caramel Apple Cheesecake

Cookies and Cream Cheesecake

CRUST

   1 cup chocolate sandwich cookie crumbs (about 12 cookies)

   1 tablespoon butter *or* margarine, melted

FILLING

   3 packages (8 ounces each) PHILADELPHIA® Cream Cheese,
      softened

   ¾ cup sugar

   1 teaspoon vanilla

   3 eggs

   16 chocolate sandwich cookies, quartered, divided

CRUST

MIX crumbs and butter; press onto bottom of 9-inch springform pan.
Bake at 325°F for 10 minutes if using a silver springform pan. (Bake at
300°F for 10 minutes if using a dark nonstick springform pan.)

FILLING

MIX cream cheese, sugar and vanilla with electric mixer on medium
speed. Add eggs; mix on low speed just until blended. Fold in 12 quartered
cookies. Pour over crust. Place remaining cookies on top of batter.

BAKE at 325°F for 50 to 55 minutes or until center is almost set if
using a silver springform pan. (Bake at 300°F if using a dark pan.) Run
knife around rim of pan to loosen cake; cool before removing rim of pan.
Refrigerate 4 hours or overnight.   *Makes 12 servings*

Prep Time: 25 minutes plus refrigerating
Bake Time: 55 minutes

Philadelphia® Fruit Smoothie Cheesecake

2 packages (8 ounces each) PHILADELPHIA® Cream Cheese, softened

1/3 cup sugar

1 cup whole strawberries, puréed

1 banana, puréed

1 tub (8 ounces) COOL WHIP® Whipped Topping, thawed

1 ready-to-use graham cracker crumb crust (6 ounces or 9 inch)

MIX cream cheese and sugar in large bowl with electric mixer on medium speed until well blended. Gently stir in puréed fruit and whipped topping.

SPOON into crust.

FREEZE 4 hours or overnight until firm. Let stand 1 hour or until cheesecake can be cut easily. Garnish with fresh strawberries.

Makes 8 servings

Take a Shortcut: After puréeing fruits, add cream cheese and sugar to food processor to avoid using another bowl.

Prep Time: 15 minutes plus freezing

Philadelphia® 3-Step® Chocolate Swirl Cheesecake

2 packages (8 ounces each) PHILADELPHIA® Cream Cheese, softened

$^1/_2$ cup sugar

$^1/_2$ teaspoon vanilla

2 eggs

1 square BAKER'S® Semi-Sweet Chocolate, melted, slightly cooled

1 ready-to-use chocolate flavor crumb crust (6 ounces or 9 inch)

MIX cream cheese, sugar and vanilla with electric mixer on medium speed until well blended. Add eggs; mix until blended. Stir melted chocolate into $^3/_4$ cup of the cream cheese batter.

POUR remaining cream cheese batter into crust. Spoon chocolate batter over cream cheese batter; cut through batter with knife several times for marble effect.

BAKE at 350°F for 35 to 40 minutes or until center is almost set. Cool. Refrigerate 3 hours or overnight.   *Makes 8 servings*

Prep Time: 10 minutes
Bake Time: 40 minutes

Philadelphia® 3-Step® Chocolate Swirl Cheesecake

Philadelphia® 3-Step® Cheesecake

2 packages (8 ounces each) PHILADELPHIA® Cream Cheese *or*
PHILADELPHIA® Neufchâtel Cheese, $1/3$ Less Fat than
Cream Cheese, softened

$1/2$ cup sugar

$1/2$ teaspoon vanilla

2 eggs

1 ready-to-use graham cracker crumb crust (6 ounces or 9 inch)

MIX cream cheese, sugar and vanilla with electric mixer on medium speed until well blended. Add eggs; mix until blended.

POUR into crust.

BAKE at 350°F for 40 minutes or until center is almost set. Cool. Refrigerate 3 hours or overnight.   *Makes 8 servings*

Fruit Topped Cheesecake: Top with 2 cups assorted cut-up fruit or 1 (21-ounce) can cherry pie filling.

Lemon Cheesecake: Stir 1 tablespoon fresh lemon juice and $1/2$ teaspoon grated lemon peel into batter.

Chocolate Chip Cheesecake: Stir $1/2$ cup miniature semi-sweet chocolate chips into batter. Sprinkle with additional $1/4$ cup chips before baking.

Prep Time: 10 minutes
Cook Time: 40 minutes

Philadelphia® 3-Step® Cheesecake

Brownie Bottom Cheesecake

1 package (10 to 20 ounces) brownie mix, any variety

3 packages (8 ounces each) PHILADELPHIA® Cream Cheese, softened

³/₄ cup sugar

1 teaspoon vanilla

¹/₂ cup BREAKSTONE'S® *or* KNUDSEN® Sour Cream

3 eggs

PREPARE and bake brownie mix as directed on package for 9-inch square pan in bottom of a well-greased 9-inch springform pan.

MIX cream cheese, sugar and vanilla with electric mixer on medium speed until well blended. Blend in sour cream. Add eggs, mixing on low speed just until blended. Pour over brownie crust.

BAKE at 325°F for 60 to 65 minutes or until center is almost set if using a silver springform pan. (Bake at 300°F for 60 to 65 minutes or until center is almost set if using a dark nonstick springform pan.) Run knife or metal spatula around rim of pan to loosen cake; cool before removing rim of pan. Refrigerate 4 hours or overnight.

Makes 12 servings

Prep Time: 20 minutes plus refrigerating
Bake Time: 65 minutes

Brownie Bottom Cheesecake

Philadelphia® 3-Step® Rocky Road Cheesecake

2 packages (8 ounces each) PHILADELPHIA® Cream Cheese, softened

$^1/_2$ cup sugar

$^1/_2$ teaspoon vanilla

2 eggs

4 squares BAKER'S® Semi-Sweet Chocolate, melted, slightly cooled

1 ready-to-use graham cracker crust (6 ounces or 9 inch)

$^1/_2$ cup miniature marshmallows

$^1/_4$ cup BAKER'S® Semi-Sweet Real Chocolate Chips

$^1/_4$ cup chopped peanuts

MIX cream cheese, sugar and vanilla at medium speed with electric mixer until well blended. Add eggs; mix until blended. Blend in melted chocolate.

POUR into crust. Sprinkle with marshmallows, chips and peanuts.

BAKE at 350°F for 40 minutes or until center is almost set. Cool. Refrigerate 3 hours or overnight. Garnish with multicolored sprinkles.

Makes 8 servings

Prep Time: 10 minutes
Bake Time: 40 minutes

Heavenly Orange Cheesecake

1 envelope unflavored gelatin

$^1/_2$ cup orange juice

3 packages (8 ounces each) PHILADELPHIA® Cream Cheese, softened

$^3/_4$ cup sugar

1 tub (12 ounces) COOL WHIP® Whipped Topping, thawed

1 tablespoon grated orange peel

1 prepared chocolate crumb crust (6 ounces or 9 inch)

SOFTEN gelatin in juice in small saucepan; stir over low heat until dissolved.

BEAT cream cheese and sugar on medium speed of electric mixer until well blended.

ADD gelatin mixture gradually, beating well after each addition. Refrigerate about 30 minutes or until slightly thickened.

GENTLY stir in whipped topping and peel; pour into crust. Refrigerate about 3 hours or until firm. Store leftover cheesecake in refrigerator.

Makes 8 servings

Prep Time: 25 minutes plus refrigerating

Philadelphia® 3-Step® Caramel Pecan Cheesecake

20 caramels

3 tablespoons milk

$^1/_2$ cup chopped pecans

1 ready-to-use graham cracker crumb crust (6 ounces or 9 inch)

2 packages (8 ounces each) PHILADELPHIA® Cream Cheese, softened

$^1/_2$ cup sugar

$^1/_2$ teaspoon vanilla

2 eggs

MICROWAVE caramels and milk in small bowl on HIGH 2 minutes or until smooth, stirring every minute. Stir in pecans; pour into crust. Refrigerate 10 minutes.

MIX cream cheese, sugar and vanilla with electric mixer on medium speed until well blended. Add eggs; mix until blended. Pour over caramel mixture.

BAKE at 350°F for 35 to 40 minutes or until center is almost set. Cool. Refrigerate 3 hours or overnight. Garnish with pecan halves and caramel sauce.   *Makes 8 servings*

Prep Time: 15 minutes plus refrigerating
Bake Time: 40 minutes

Philadelphia® 3-Step® Caramel Pecan Cheesecake

Dazzling Desserts

There's more to cream cheese than just cheesecakes! How about rich, decadent fudge, cookies or truffles? Flip through these recipes and see how deliciously versatile cream cheese really is!

Cherries in the Snow

1 package (8 ounces) PHILADELPHIA® Cream Cheese, softened
$^1/_2$ cup sugar
2 cups thawed COOL WHIP® Whipped Topping
1 can (20 ounces) cherry pie filling, divided

MIX cream cheese and sugar in large bowl until smooth. Gently stir in whipped topping.

LAYER $^1/_4$ cup cream cheese mixture and 2 tablespoons pie filling in each of 4 stemmed glasses or bowls. Repeat layers.   *Makes 4 servings*

Prep Time: 10 minutes

Creamy Lemon Bars

1 package (2-layer size) lemon cake mix

3 large eggs, divided

$^1/_2$ cup oil

2 packages (8 ounces each) PHILADELPHIA® Cream Cheese, softened

1 container (8 ounces) BREAKSTONE'S® *or* KNUDSEN® Sour Cream

$^1/_2$ cup granulated sugar

1 teaspoon grated lemon peel

1 tablespoon lemon juice

Powdered sugar

MIX cake mix, 1 egg and oil. Press mixture onto bottom and up sides of lightly greased 15×10×1-inch baking pan. Bake at 350°F for 10 minutes.

BEAT cream cheese with electric mixer on medium speed until smooth. Add remaining 2 eggs, sour cream, granulated sugar, peel and juice; mix until blended. Pour batter into crust.

BAKE at 350°F for 30 to 35 minutes or until filling is just set in center and edges are light golden brown. Cool. Sprinkle with powdered sugar. Cut into bars. Store leftover bars in refrigerator.   *Makes 2 dozen bars*

Prep Time: 15 minutes
Bake Time: 35 minutes

Creamy Lemon Bars

Philadelphia® Sugar Cookies

1 package (8 ounces) PHILADELPHIA® Cream Cheese, softened

1 cup (2 sticks) butter *or* margarine, softened

²/₃ cup sugar

¹/₄ teaspoon vanilla

2 cups flour

Colored sugar, sprinkles and colored gels

BEAT cream cheese, butter, ²/₃ cup sugar and vanilla with electric mixer on medium speed until well blended. Mix in flour. Refrigerate several hours or overnight.

ROLL dough to ¹/₄-inch thickness on lightly floured surface. Cut into desired shapes; sprinkle with colored sugar. Place on ungreased cookie sheets.

BAKE at 350°F for 12 to 15 minutes or until edges are lightly browned. Cool on wire racks. Decorate as desired with colored sugar, sprinkles and colored gels.   *Makes 3¹/₂ dozen*

Prep Time: 10 minutes plus refrigerating
Bake Time: 15 minutes

To soften butter quickly, place 1 stick of butter on a microwavable plate and heat at LOW (30% power) about 30 seconds or just until softened.

Philadelphia® Sugar Cookies

Cheesecake Cream Dip

1 package (8 ounces) PHILADELPHIA® Cream Cheese, softened
1 jar (7 ounces) marshmallow cream

MIX cream cheese and marshmallow cream until well blended.
Refrigerate.

SERVE with assorted cut-up fruit, pound cake or cookies.

Makes 1 1/2 cups

Prep Time: 5 minutes plus refrigerating

Cheesecake Cream Dip

Chocolate Peanut Butter Bars

1½ cups chocolate-covered graham cracker crumbs (about
      17 crackers)
  3 tablespoons butter *or* margarine, melted
  1 package (8 ounces) PHILADELPHIA® Cream Cheese, softened
½ cup crunchy peanut butter
  1 cup powdered sugar
  2 squares BAKER'S® Semi-Sweet Baking Chocolate
  1 teaspoon butter *or* margarine

MIX crumbs and 3 tablespoons melted butter. Press onto bottom of
9-inch square baking pan. Bake at 350°F for 20 minutes. Cool.

BEAT cream cheese, peanut butter and sugar with electric mixer on
medium speed until well blended. Spoon over crust.

MICROWAVE chocolate with 1 teaspoon butter on HIGH 1 to
2 minutes or until chocolate begins to melt, stirring halfway through
heating time. Stir until chocolate is completely melted. Drizzle over
cream cheese mixture.

REFRIGERATE 6 hours or overnight. Cut into squares. Store in
airtight container in refrigerator. *Makes 18 servings*

Prep Time: 20 minutes
Bake Time: 20 minutes

Philadelphia® Cheesecake Brownies

1 package (19.8 ounces) brownie mix (do not use mix that
        includes syrup pouch)
1 package (8 ounces) PHILADELPHIA® Cream Cheese, softened
¹/₃ cup sugar
1 egg
¹/₂ teaspoon vanilla

PREPARE brownie mix as directed on package. Pour into greased
13×9-inch baking pan.

BEAT cream cheese with electric mixer on medium speed until smooth.
Mix in sugar until blended. Add egg and vanilla; mix just until blended.
Pour cream cheese mixture over brownie batter; cut through batter with
knife several times for marble effect.

BAKE at 350°F for 35 to 40 minutes or until cream cheese mixture is
lightly browned. Cool. Cut into squares.   *Makes 2 dozen brownies*

Special Extras: For extra chocolate flavor, sprinkle 1 cup BAKER'S®
Semi-Sweet Real Chocolate Chips over top of brownies before baking.

Prep Time: 20 minutes
Bake Time: 40 minutes

Philadelphia® Cheesecake Brownies

Peachy Berry Dessert

$^1/_2$ cup plus 1 tablespoon sugar

$^1/_2$ teaspoon ground cinnamon

$^1/_2$ package (15 ounces) refrigerated pie crust

1 tablespoon butter *or* margarine, melted

2 cans (15 ounces each) peach slices in juice

2 packages (8 ounces each) PHILADELPHIA® Cream Cheese, softened

1 tub (12 ounces) COOL WHIP® Whipped Topping, thawed

$^1/_2$ cup blueberries

HEAT oven to 400°F.

STIR 1 tablespoon sugar and cinnamon together in small bowl. Unfold crust; cut into 10 to 12 wedges. Place pastry wedges on cookie sheet, $^1/_2$ inch apart. Brush with melted butter and sprinkle with sugar mixture. Bake 8 to 10 minutes or until lightly browned. Remove to wire rack; cool.

DRAIN peaches, reserving $^1/_2$ cup juice. Beat cream cheese and remaining $^1/_2$ cup sugar in large bowl with wire whisk until smooth. Gradually beat in reserved juice. Fold in $4^1/_2$ cups whipped topping. Spoon into shallow bowl. Top with remaining whipped topping, peaches and blueberries.

ARRANGE pastry wedges in pinwheel fashion on top.

Makes 10 to 12 servings

Variation: 3 cups fresh sliced peaches and $^1/_2$ cup peach nectar may be substituted for canned peaches.

Prep Time: 15 minutes

Chocolate Fudge

4 cups sifted powdered sugar
1 package (8 ounces) PHILADELPHIA® Cream Cheese, softened
4 squares BAKER'S® Unsweetened Baking Chocolate, melted
½ cup chopped nuts
1 teaspoon vanilla

ADD sugar gradually to cream cheese, beating with electric mixer on medium speed until well blended. Mix in remaining ingredients.

SPREAD into greased 8-inch square pan. Refrigerate several hours.

CUT into 1-inch squares. Refrigerate leftover fudge.

Makes 64 squares

Peppermint Fudge: Omit nuts and vanilla. Stir ¼ cup crushed peppermint candies and few drops peppermint extract into cream cheese mixture before spreading into pan. Sprinkle with additional ¼ cup crushed peppermint candies. Refrigerate and cut as directed.

Prep Time: 15 minutes plus refrigerating

Apple Cranberry Pie

1 package (8 ounces) PHILADELPHIA® Cream Cheese, softened
$^1/_2$ cup firmly packed brown sugar, divided
1 egg
1 (9-inch) unbaked pastry shell
2 cups sliced apples
$^1/_2$ cup halved cranberries
1 teaspoon ground cinnamon, divided
$^1/_3$ cup flour
$^1/_3$ cup old-fashioned *or* quick-cooking oats, uncooked
$^1/_4$ cup ($^1/_2$ stick) butter *or* margarine
$^1/_4$ cup chopped nuts

MIX cream cheese and $^1/_4$ cup of the sugar with electric mixer on medium speed until well blended. Blend in egg. Pour into pastry shell.

TOSS apples, cranberries and $^1/_2$ teaspoon cinnamon. Spoon over cream cheese mixture.

MIX flour, oats, remaining $^1/_4$ cup sugar and remaining $^1/_2$ teaspoon cinnamon. Cut in butter until mixture resembles coarse crumbs. Stir in nuts. Spoon over fruit mixture.

BAKE at 375°F for 40 to 45 minutes or until lightly browned. Cool slightly before serving. *Makes 8 to 10 servings*

Prep Time: 15 minutes plus cooling
Bake Time: 45 minutes

Apple Cranberry Pie

Cherry Cheesecake Squares

2 cups graham cracker crumbs

$^1/_4$ cup sugar

$^1/_4$ cup ($^1/_2$ stick) butter *or* margarine, melted

3 packages (8 ounces each) PHILADELPHIA® Cream Cheese, softened

$^3/_4$ cup sugar

1 teaspoon vanilla

2 eggs

1 can (20 ounces) cherry pie filling

MIX crumbs, $^1/_4$ cup sugar and butter. Press into 13×9-inch baking pan. Bake at 325°F for 10 minutes.

MIX cream cheese, $^3/_4$ cup sugar and vanilla with electric mixer on medium speed until well blended. Add eggs; mix just until blended. Pour over crust.

BAKE at 325°F for 35 minutes or until center is almost set. Cool. Refrigerate 3 hours or overnight. Top with pie filling. Cut into squares.

Makes 18 servings

Prep Time: 20 minutes plus refrigerating
Bake Time: 35 minutes

Cherry Cheesecake Squares

Philadelphia® Snowmen Cookies

1 package (8 ounces) PHILADELPHIA® Cream Cheese, softened
1 cup powdered sugar
3/4 cup (1 1/2 sticks) butter *or* margarine
1/2 teaspoon vanilla
2 1/4 cups flour
1/2 teaspoon baking soda
    Sifted powdered sugar
    Miniature peanut butter cups (optional)

MIX cream cheese, 1 cup sugar, butter and vanilla with electric mixer on medium speed until well blended. Add flour and baking soda; mix well.

SHAPE dough into equal number of 1/2-inch and 1-inch diameter balls. Using 1 small and 1 large ball for each snowman, place balls, slightly overlapping, on ungreased cookie sheets. Flatten to 1/4-inch thickness with bottom of glass dipped in additional flour. Repeat with remaining balls.

BAKE at 325°F for 19 to 21 minutes or until light golden brown. Cool on wire racks. Sprinkle each snowman with sifted powdered sugar. Decorate with icing as desired. Cut peanut butter cups in half for hats.

Makes about 3 dozen cookies

Prep Time: 20 minutes
Bake Time: 21 minutes

Philadelphia® Snowmen Cookies

Frosted Pumpkin Squares

CAKE

3/4 cup (1 1/2 sticks) butter *or* margarine

2 cups granulated sugar

1 can (16 ounces) pumpkin

4 eggs

2 cups flour

2 teaspoons CALUMET® Baking Powder

1 teaspoon ground cinnamon

1/2 teaspoon baking soda

1/2 teaspoon salt

1/4 teaspoon ground nutmeg

1 cup chopped walnuts

FROSTING

1 package (8 ounces) PHILADELPHIA® Cream Cheese, softened

1/3 cup butter *or* margarine

1 teaspoon vanilla

3 cups sifted powdered sugar

CAKE

MIX butter and sugar with electric mixer on medium speed until light and fluffy. Blend in pumpkin and eggs. Mix in combined dry ingredients. Stir in walnuts.

SPREAD into greased and floured 15×10×1-inch baking pan.

BAKE at 350°F for 30 to 35 minutes or until wooden pick inserted in center comes out clean; cool.

FROSTING

MIX cream cheese, butter and vanilla in large bowl with electric mixer until creamy. Gradually add sugar, mixing well after each addition. Spread onto cake. Cut into squares.   *Makes 2 dozen squares*

Prep Time: 20 minutes
Bake Time: 35 minutes

Frosted Pumpkin Square

Magic Dip

1 package (8 ounces) PHILADELPHIA® Cream Cheese, softened
1 cup BAKER'S® Semi-Sweet Real Chocolate Chips
$^1/_2$ cup BAKER'S® ANGEL FLAKE® Coconut, toasted
$^1/_2$ cup chopped peanuts
  Graham crackers

SPREAD cream cheese onto bottom of 9-inch microwavable pie plate or quiche dish.

TOP with chocolate chips, coconut and peanuts.

MICROWAVE on MEDIUM (50% power) 3 to 4 minutes or until warm. Serve with graham crackers. Garnish, if desired.

Makes 6 to 8 servings

Prep Time: 5 minutes
Microwave Time: 4 minutes

*Make this dip extra fun for kids—serve it with
animal crackers or bear-shaped graham cookies. It
can also be divided into individual portions and
served in small cups or ramekins.*

Magic Dip

Truffle Treats

6 squares BAKER'S® Semi-Sweet Baking Chocolate

¹/₄ cup (¹/₂ stick) margarine

2²/₃ cups (7 ounces) BAKER'S® ANGEL FLAKE® Coconut

1 package (8 ounces) PHILADELPHIA® Cream Cheese, softened

2¹/₂ cups cold half-and-half *or* milk

1 package (6-serving size) JELL-O® Chocolate Flavor Instant
    Pudding & Pie Filling

2 tablespoons unsweetened cocoa

1 tablespoon powdered sugar

PLACE chocolate in heavy saucepan over very low heat; stir constantly until just melted. Remove 2 tablespoons of the melted chocolate; set aside.

STIR margarine into remaining chocolate in saucepan until melted. Gradually stir in coconut, tossing to coat evenly. Press mixture into 13×9-inch baking pan which has been lined with foil.

BEAT cream cheese at medium speed of electric mixer until smooth; beat in reserved 2 tablespoons chocolate. Gradually mix in half-and-half. Add pudding mix. Beat at low speed until well blended, about 1 minute. Pour over crust. Freeze until firm, about 4 hours or overnight.

MIX together cocoa and sugar in small bowl; sift over truffle mixture. Lift with foil from pan onto cutting board; let stand 10 minutes to soften slightly. Cut into diamonds, squares or triangles.

Makes about 20 pieces

Prep Time: 15 minutes plus freezing

Shortbread Cookies

1^1/$_2$ cups (3 sticks) butter *or* margarine, softened

1 package (8 ounces) PHILADELPHIA® Cream Cheese, softened

^{1}/$_2$ cup granulated sugar

3 cups flour

Powdered sugar

MIX butter, cream cheese and granulated sugar until well blended. Mix in flour.

SHAPE dough into 1-inch balls; place on ungreased cookie sheets.

BAKE at 400°F for 10 to 13 minutes or until light golden brown and set; cool on wire racks. Sprinkle with powdered sugar.

Makes about 6 dozen cookies

Holiday Cookies: Tint dough with a few drops of food coloring before shaping to add a festive touch.

Prep Time: 15 minutes
Bake Time: 13 minutes

Praline Bars

3/4 cup butter *or* margarine, softened

1 cup sugar, divided

1 teaspoon vanilla, divided

1 1/2 cups flour

2 packages (8 ounces each) PHILADELPHIA® Cream Cheese, softened

2 eggs

1/2 cup almond brickle chips

3 tablespoons caramel ice cream topping

MIX butter, 1/2 cup of the sugar and 1/2 teaspoon of the vanilla with electric mixer on medium speed until light and fluffy. Gradually add flour, mixing on low speed until blended. Press onto bottom of 13×9-inch pan. Bake at 350°F for 20 to 23 minutes or until lightly browned.

MIX cream cheese, remaining 1/2 cup sugar and 1/2 teaspoon vanilla with electric mixer on medium speed until well blended. Add eggs; mix well. Blend in chips. Pour over crust. Dot top of cream cheese mixture with topping. Cut through batter with knife several times for marble effect.

BAKE at 350°F for 30 minutes. Cool in pan on wire rack. Cut into bars. *Makes 2 dozen bars*

Prep Time: 30 minutes
Bake Time: 30 minutes

Praline Bars

Special Occasions

When you need a showstopping dessert, look no further than this chapter! An extra-special cheesecake, trifle, tiramisu or chocolate cake is certain to make any meal a memorable one.

Chocolate Truffles

3 cups sifted powdered sugar

1 package (8 ounces) PHILADELPHIA® Cream Cheese, softened

1 package (12 ounces) BAKER'S® Semi-Sweet Real Chocolate
  Chips, melted

1 tablespoon coffee-flavored liqueur

1 tablespoon orange-flavored liqueur

1 tablespoon almond-flavored liqueur

  Ground nuts, powdered sugar, nonpareils *or* unsweetened cocoa

  Powdered sugar

  Unsweetened cocoa

ADD 3 cups powdered sugar gradually to cream cheese, beating with electric mixer on medium speed until well blended. Add melted chocolate; mix well.

DIVIDE mixture into thirds. Add different flavor liqueur to each third; mix well. Refrigerate several hours.

SHAPE mixture into 1-inch balls. Roll in nuts, sugar, nonpareils or cocoa. Refrigerate.   *Makes 5 dozen truffles*

Microwave Tip: Place chips in medium microwavable bowl. Microwave on HIGH 1 to 2 minutes or until chips begin to melt, stirring every minute. Remove from oven. Stir until completely melted.

Prep Time: 20 minutes plus refrigerating

101

Philadelphia® 3-Step® Pralines and Cream Cheesecake

2 packages (8 ounces each) PHILADELPHIA® Cream Cheese,
   softened

¹/₂ cup sugar

¹/₂ teaspoon vanilla

2 eggs

¹/₂ cup almond brickle chips

1 ready-to-use graham cracker crust (6 ounces or 9 inch)

3 tablespoons caramel ice cream topping

MIX cream cheese, sugar and vanilla at medium speed with electric mixer until well blended. Add eggs; mix until blended. Blend in almond brickle chips.

POUR into crust. Dot top of cheesecake batter with topping. Cut through batter with knife several times for marble effect.

BAKE at 350°F for 40 minutes or until center is almost set. Cool. Refrigerate 3 hours or overnight. *Makes 8 servings*

Prep Time: 10 minutes
Bake Time: 40 minutes

Philadelphia® 3-Step® Pralines and Cream Cheesecake

Easy English Trifle

1 package (8 ounces) PHILADELPHIA® Cream Cheese, softened

2 cups milk, divided

1 package (4-serving size) JELL-O® Vanilla Flavor Instant
    Pudding & Pie Filling

2$\frac{1}{2}$ cups cubed pound cake

$\frac{1}{2}$ cup strawberry preserves

1 can (16 ounces) peach slices, drained, chopped

MIX cream cheese and $\frac{1}{2}$ cup milk in large bowl with electric mixer on medium speed until well blended. Add pudding mix and remaining 1$\frac{1}{2}$ cups milk; beat on low speed 1 minute.

LAYER $\frac{1}{2}$ of the cake, preserves, peach slices and pudding mixture in 1$\frac{1}{2}$-quart serving bowl; repeat layers. Cover surface with wax paper or plastic wrap; refrigerate.   *Makes 8 servings*

Prep Time: 15 minutes plus refrigerating

Customize this trifle with your favorite ingredients—
try different flavors of pudding and preserves, or
substitute angel food cake, sponge cake, ladyfingers
or even chocolate cake for the pound cake.

Easy English Trifle

Philadelphia® Tiramisu

1 package (10³/₄ ounces) frozen pound cake, thawed, thinly sliced, divided

1 cup double strength MAXWELL HOUSE® Coffee, divided

2 packages (8 ounces each) PHILADELPHIA® Cream Cheese, softened

¹/₂ cup sugar

2 tablespoons almond-flavored liqueur (optional)

2 cups thawed COOL WHIP® Whipped Topping

1 teaspoon unsweetened cocoa

ARRANGE ¹/₂ of the pound cake slices on bottom of 13×9-inch dish; drizzle with ¹/₂ cup of the coffee.

MIX cream cheese, sugar and liqueur with electric mixer on medium speed until well blended. Gently stir in whipped topping.

SPOON ¹/₂ of the cream cheese mixture over pound cake in baking dish. Top with remaining pound cake; drizzle with remaining ¹/₂ cup coffee. Spoon remaining cream cheese mixture over pound cake. Sprinkle with cocoa. Refrigerate several hours or overnight. Store leftover dessert in refrigerator.   *Makes 12 to 16 servings*

Tip: Substitute ¹/₂ teaspoon almond extract for the almond flavored liqueur.

Prep Time: 15 minutes plus refrigerating

Philadelphia® 3-Step® Triple Chocolate Layer Cheesecake

2 packages (8 ounces each) PHILADELPHIA® Cream Cheese, softened

$^{1}/_{2}$ cup sugar

$^{1}/_{2}$ teaspoon vanilla

2 eggs

3 squares BAKER'S® Semi-Sweet Baking Chocolate, melted, slightly cooled

4 squares BAKER'S® Premium White Baking Chocolate, melted, slightly cooled

1 ready-to-use chocolate flavor crumb crust (6 ounces or 9 inch)

MIX cream cheese, sugar and vanilla with electric mixer on medium speed until well blended. Add eggs; mix until blended. Stir melted semi-sweet chocolate into 1 cup of the batter. Stir melted white chocolate into remaining plain batter.

POUR semi-sweet chocolate batter into crust. Top with white chocolate batter.

BAKE at 350°F for 35 to 40 minutes or until center is almost set. Cool. Refrigerate 3 hours or overnight. _Makes 8 servings_

Prep Time: 10 minutes plus refrigerating
Bake Time: 40 minutes

Eggnog Cheesecake

CRUST

    2 cups vanilla wafer crumbs

    6 tablespoons butter or margarine, melted

    $1/2$ teaspoon ground nutmeg

FILLING

    4 packages (8 ounces each) PHILADELPHIA® Cream Cheese,
      softened

    1 cup sugar

    3 tablespoons flour

    3 tablespoons rum

    1 teaspoon vanilla

    2 eggs

    1 cup whipping cream

    4 egg yolks

HEAT oven to 325°F.

CRUST

MIX crumbs, butter and nutmeg; press onto bottom and $1 1/2$ inches up sides of 9-inch springform pan. Bake 10 minutes.

FILLING

BEAT cream cheese, sugar, flour, rum and vanilla at medium speed with electric mixer until well blended. Add eggs, 1 at a time, mixing at low speed after each addition, just until blended.

BLEND in cream and egg yolks; pour into crust.

BAKE 1 hour and 10 minutes to 1 hour and 15 minutes or until center is almost set. Run knife or metal spatula around rim of pan to loosen cake; cool before removing rim of pan. Refrigerate 4 hours or overnight. Garnish with COOL WHIP® Whipped Topping and ground nutmeg.

Makes 12 servings

Prep Time: 25 minutes
Bake Time: 1 hour 15 minutes

Eggnog Cheesecake

Chocolate-Chocolate Cake

1 package (8 ounces) PHILADELPHIA® Cream Cheese, softened

1 cup BREAKSTONE'S® or KNUDSEN® Sour Cream

$^{1}/_{2}$ cup coffee-flavored liqueur or water

2 eggs

1 package (2-layer size) chocolate cake mix

1 package (4-serving size) JELL-O® Chocolate Flavor Instant
   Pudding & Pie Filling

1 cup BAKER'S® Semi-Sweet Real Chocolate Chips

MIX cream cheese, sour cream, liqueur and eggs with electric mixer on medium speed until well blended. Add cake mix and pudding mix; beat until well blended. Fold in chips. (Batter will be stiff.)

POUR into greased and floured 12-cup fluted tube pan.

BAKE at 325°F for 1 hour to 1 hour and 5 minutes or until toothpick inserted near center comes out clean. Cool 5 minutes. Remove from pan. Cool completely on wire rack. Sprinkle with powdered sugar before serving. Garnish, if desired.   *Makes 10 to 12 servings*

Prep Time: 10 minutes plus cooling

Bake Time: 1 hour 5 minutes

Chocolate-Chocolate Cake

Pumpkin Marble Cheesecake

CRUST

   2 cups gingersnap cookie crumbs
   $^1/_2$ cup finely chopped pecans
   6 tablespoons butter *or* margarine, melted

FILLING

   3 packages (8 ounces each) PHILADELPHIA® Cream Cheese,
      softened
   1 cup sugar, divided
   1 teaspoon vanilla
   3 eggs
   1 cup canned pumpkin
   1 teaspoon ground cinnamon
   $^1/_4$ teaspoon ground nutmeg
      Dash ground cloves

CRUST

MIX crumbs, pecans and butter; press onto bottom and 2 inches up side
of 9-inch springform pan.

FILLING

MIX cream cheese, $^3/_4$ cup of the sugar and vanilla with electric mixer on
medium speed until well blended. Add eggs, mixing on low speed just until
blended. Reserve $1^1/_2$ cups batter. Add remaining $^1/_4$ cup sugar, pumpkin
and spices to remaining batter; mix well. Spoon $^1/_2$ of the pumpkin batter
over crust; top with spoonfuls of plain batter. Repeat layers. Cut through
batter with knife several times for marble effect.

BAKE at 325°F for 55 minutes or until center is almost set if using a silver springform pan. (Bake at 300°F for 55 minutes or until center is almost set if using a dark nonstick springform pan.) Run knife or metal spatula around rim of pan to loosen cake; cool before removing rim of pan. Refrigerate 4 hours or overnight. *Makes 12 servings*

Prep Time: 25 minutes plus refrigerating
Bake Time: 55 minutes

Pumpkin Marble Cheesecake

Philadelphia® 3-Step® Black Forest Cherry Cheesecake

2 packages (8 ounces each) PHILADELPHIA® Cream Cheese, softened

$^1/_2$ cup sugar

$^1/_2$ teaspoon vanilla

2 eggs

4 squares BAKER'S® Semi-Sweet Chocolate, melted, slightly cooled

1 ready-to-use chocolate flavor crumb crust (6 ounces or 9 inch)

1 cup thawed COOL WHIP® Whipped Topping

1$^1/_2$ cups cherry pie filling

MIX cream cheese, sugar and vanilla with electric mixer on medium speed until well blended. Add eggs; mix until blended. Stir in melted chocolate.

POUR into crust.

BAKE at 350°F for 35 to 40 minutes or until center is almost set. Cool. Refrigerate 3 hours or overnight. Spread whipped topping over chilled cheesecake; cover with pie filling.   *Makes 8 servings*

Prep Time: 10 minutes
Bake Time: 40 minutes

Unlike milk chocolate, semisweet and bittersweet chocolate contain no milk solids and can last for years if stored properly, in a cool, dry place.

Philadelphia® 3-Step® Black Forest Cherry Cheesecake

Raspberry Cream Pie

1 package (8 ounces) PHILADELPHIA® Cream Cheese, softened
¾ cup raspberry fruit spread
⅓ cup cold milk
1 package (4-serving size) JELL-O® Vanilla Flavor Instant
    Pudding & Pie Filling
1 tub (8 ounces) COOL WHIP® Whipped Topping, thawed
    Red food coloring (8 to 10 drops)
1 prepared chocolate flavor crumb crust (6 ounces or 9 inch)

BEAT cream cheese and fruit spread in large bowl with wire whisk until smooth. Gradually beat in milk until smooth. Add pudding mix. Beat 2 minutes. Reserve ½ cup whipped topping. Gently stir remaining whipped topping into pudding mixture. Stir in food coloring until desired color is achieved. Spoon into crust.

REFRIGERATE 3 hours. Garnish with remaining whipped topping.

Makes 8 servings

Prep Time: 10 minutes

116

Philadelphia® Strawberry Layer Cheesecake

2 packages (8 ounces each) PHILADELPHIA® Cream Cheese, softened
$^1/_2$ cup sugar
$^1/_2$ teaspoon vanilla
2 eggs
$^1/_4$ cup strawberry preserves
5 drops red food coloring
1 ready-to-use graham cracker crumb crust (6 ounces or 9 inch)

MIX cream cheese, sugar and vanilla with electric mixer on medium speed until well blended. Add eggs; mix until blended. Blend preserves and food coloring into 1 cup of the batter.

POUR strawberry batter into crust. Top with plain batter.

BAKE at 350°F for 40 minutes or until center is almost set. Cool. Refrigerate 3 hours or overnight. Refrigerate leftover cheesecake.

Makes 8 servings

Springform Pan: Mix $1^1/_2$ cups graham cracker crumbs, 3 tablespoons sugar and $^1/_3$ cup butter, melted; press onto bottom of 9-inch springform pan. Double ingredients in recipe for batter. Mix and layer over crust as directed. Bake at 350°F for 55 minutes or until center is almost set. Loosen cake from rim of pan; cool before removing rim of pan.

Prep Time: 10 minutes plus refrigerating
Bake Time: 40 minutes

Cappuccino Cream

1 package (8 ounces) PHILADELPHIA® Cream Cheese, softened

1 cup brewed strong MAXWELL HOUSE® Coffee, at room temperature

$^{1}/_{2}$ cup milk

1 package (4-serving size) JELL-O® Brand Vanilla Flavor Instant Pudding & Pie Filling

$^{1}/_{4}$ teaspoon ground cinnamon

1 tub (8 ounces) COOL WHIP® Whipped Topping, thawed, divided

Cookies, such as chocolate-laced pirouettes *or* biscotti

MIX cream cheese with electric mixer on medium speed until smooth. Gradually add coffee and milk, beating until well blended. Add pudding mix and cinnamon. Beat on low speed 2 minutes. Let stand 5 minutes or until thickened.

STIR in 2 cups of the whipped topping. Spoon mixture into 6 dessert glasses or 1-quart serving bowl.

REFRIGERATE until ready to serve. Just before serving, top with remaining whipped topping. Serve with cookies.   *Makes 6 servings*

Prep Time: 20 minutes plus refrigerating

Cappuccino Cream

Chocolate Truffle Cheesecake

CRUST

1 1/2 cups crushed chocolate sandwich cookies (about 18 cookies)

2 tablespoons butter *or* margarine, melted

FILLING

3 packages (8 ounces each) PHILADELPHIA® Cream Cheese, softened

1 cup sugar

1 teaspoon vanilla

8 squares BAKER'S® Semi-Sweet Baking Chocolate, melted, slightly cooled

1/4 cup hazelnut liqueur (optional)

3 eggs

CRUST

MIX crumbs and butter; press onto bottom of 9-inch springform pan. Bake at 325°F for 10 minutes if using a silver springform pan. (Bake at 300°F for 10 minutes if using a dark nonstick springform pan.)

FILLING

MIX cream cheese, sugar and vanilla with electric mixer on medium speed until well blended. Blend in melted chocolate and liqueur. Add eggs, mixing on low speed just until blended. Pour over crust.

BAKE at 325°F for 55 to 60 minutes or until center is almost set if using a silver springform pan. (Bake at 300°F for 55 to 60 minutes if using a dark nonstick springform pan.) Run knife or metal spatula around rim of pan to loosen cake; cool before removing rim of pan. Refrigerate 4 hours or overnight. *Makes 12 servings*

Chocolate Truffle Cheesecake

Philadelphia® 3-Step® Toffee Crunch Cheesecake

2 packages (8 ounces each) PHILADELPHIA® Cream Cheese, softened

½ cup firmly packed brown sugar

½ teaspoon vanilla

2 eggs

4 packages (1.4 ounces each) chocolate-covered English toffee bars, chopped (1 cup), divided

1 ready-to-use graham cracker crumb crust (6 ounces or 9 inch)

MIX cream cheese, sugar and vanilla with electric mixer on medium speed until well blended. Add eggs; mix until blended. Stir in ¾ cup of the chopped toffee bars.

POUR into crust. Sprinkle with remaining toffee bars.

BAKE at 350°F for 35 to 40 minutes or until center is almost set. Cool. Refrigerate 3 hours or overnight.   *Makes 8 servings*

Prep Time: 10 minutes
Bake Time: 40 minutes

METRIC CONVERSION CHART

VOLUME MEASUREMENTS (dry)

1/8 teaspoon = 0.5 mL
1/4 teaspoon = 1 mL
1/2 teaspoon = 2 mL
3/4 teaspoon = 4 mL
1 teaspoon = 5 mL
1 tablespoon = 15 mL
2 tablespoons = 30 mL
1/4 cup = 60 mL
1/3 cup = 75 mL
1/2 cup = 125 mL
2/3 cup = 150 mL
3/4 cup = 175 mL
1 cup = 250 mL
2 cups = 1 pint = 500 mL
3 cups = 750 mL
4 cups = 1 quart = 1 L

VOLUME MEASUREMENTS (fluid)

1 fluid ounce (2 tablespoons) = 30 mL
4 fluid ounces (1/2 cup) = 125 mL
8 fluid ounces (1 cup) = 250 mL
12 fluid ounces (1 1/2 cups) = 375 mL
16 fluid ounces (2 cups) = 500 mL

WEIGHTS (mass)

1/2 ounce = 15 g
1 ounce = 30 g
3 ounces = 90 g
4 ounces = 120 g
8 ounces = 225 g
10 ounces = 285 g
12 ounces = 360 g
16 ounces = 1 pound = 450 g

DIMENSIONS

1/16 inch = 2 mm
1/8 inch = 3 mm
1/4 inch = 6 mm
1/2 inch = 1.5 cm
3/4 inch = 2 cm
1 inch = 2.5 cm

OVEN TEMPERATURES

250°F = 120°C
275°F = 140°C
300°F = 150°C
325°F = 160°C
350°F = 180°C
375°F = 190°C
400°F = 200°C
425°F = 220°C
450°F = 230°C

BAKING PAN SIZES

Utensil	Size in Inches/Quarts	Metric Volume	Size in Centimeters
Baking or Cake Pan (square or rectangular)	8×8×2	2 L	20×20×5
	9×9×2	2.5 L	23×23×5
	12×8×2	3 L	30×20×5
	13×9×2	3.5 L	33×23×5
Loaf Pan	8×4×3	1.5 L	20×10×7
	9×5×3	2 L	23×13×7
Round Layer Cake Pan	8×1½	1.2 L	20×4
	9×1½	1.5 L	23×4
Pie Plate	8×1¼	750 mL	20×3
	9×1¼	1 L	23×3
Baking Dish or Casserole	1 quart	1 L	—
	1½ quart	1.5 L	—
	2 quart	2 L	—